It's fun to draw
Pets

Mark Bergin

Sky Pony Press
New York

Author:
Mark Bergin was born in Hastings, England. He has illustrated an award-winning series and written over twenty books. He has done many book designs, layouts, and storyboards in many styles including cartoon for numerous books, posters, and adverts. He lives in Bexhill-on-sea with his wife and three children.

HOW TO USE THIS BOOK:
Start by following the numbered splats on the left-hand page. These steps will ask you to add some lines to your drawing. The new lines are always drawn in red so you can see how the drawing builds from step to step. Read the "You can do it!" splats to learn about drawing and shading techniques you can use.

Sky Pony Press books may be purchased in bulk at special discounts for sales promotion, corporate gifts, fund-raising, or educational purposes. Special editions can also be created to specifications. For details, contact the Special Sales Department, Sky Pony Press, 307 West 36th Street, 11th Floor, New York, NY 10018 or info@skyhorsepublishing.com.

Sky Pony® is a registered trademark of Skyhorse Publishing, Inc.®, a Delaware corporation.

Visit our website at www.skyponypress.com.

10 9 8 7 6 5 4 3 2 1

Manufactured in China, September 2013
This product conforms to CPSIA 2008

Bergin, Mark, 1961-
[Pets]
It's fun to draw pets / Mark Bergin.
pages cm
Summary: "A first drawing book for kids teaching them step-by-step ways to draw their favorite pets"-- Provided by publisher.
ISBN 978-1-62636-385-4 (trade pbk.)
1. Animals in art--Juvenile literature. 2. Drawing--Technique--Juvenile literature. I. Title.
NC783.8.P48B48 2014
743.6--dc23
2013034496

ISBN: 978-1-62636-385-4

Contents

Cat

1 Start by drawing this shape for the head.

2 Add an ear, nose, eye, mouth, and whiskers.

3 Draw in a bean-shaped body.

you can do it!

Use a felt-tip marker for the lines and add color using colored pencils.

4 Add two back legs and a belly shape.

splat-a-fact

Cats sleep for 16-18 hours a day.

5 Draw in two front legs and a tail.

Dog

2 Draw in the ears, and add a bone in the dog's mouth.

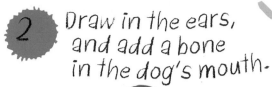

you can do it!

Use crayons to add color and a felt-tip marker for the lines.

1 Start with an oval for the head. Add cheeks and eyes.

4 Draw in the back legs and the tail.

3 Add an oval for the body.

splat-a-fact

Dogs have better hearing than humans and can hear sounds at four times the distance.

5 Draw in the front legs, and add a collar.

Fish

1 Start by drawing the body shape.

Splat-a-fact

Fish sleep with their eyes open!

2 Add a curved line for the face. Draw in the mouth and a dot for the eye.

3 Add a tail and two fins.

4 Draw in the striped markings.

9

Parakeet

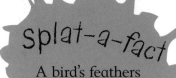

1 Start with the head. Add a beak and a dot for the eye.

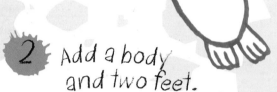
2 Add a body and two feet.

3 Draw in the tail feathers.

4 Add the wings.

you can do it!

Use oil pastels and smudge them with your finger. Use a felt-tip marker for the lines.

Guinea pig

you can do it!
Cut out the shapes from colored paper and glue in place. The guinea pig head must overlap the body. Use felt-tip marker for the lines.

1 Start by cutting out a curvy shape for the body. Glue it down.

2 Cut out the head shape with tufts of hair. Glue down.

4 Cut out four feet and brown fur for the guinea pig's back. Glue down.

3 Cut out a brown patch for the face. Glue it down. Cut out an ear and glue down. Draw in the eye and nose.

Splat-a-fact
A group of guinea pigs is called a herd.

MAKE SURE YOU GET AN ADULT TO HELP YOU WHEN USING SCISSORS!

13

Horse

you can do it!

Use crayons to create various textures. Paint over with watercolor paint. Use a felt-tip marker for the lines.

1 Start by drawing a bean-shaped body.

2 Draw in a neck and a head. Add dots for the eyes and nostrils.

3 Draw in four legs with hooves.

splat-a-fact

Male foals are called colts and female foals are called fillies.

4 Add a tail and a mane. Draw in ears and spots on the body. Add a piece of grass to the mouth.

Lizard

1 Start with this shape for the head.

2 Add two circles with dots for the eyes, a mouth, and dots for the nostrils.

you can do it!

Use a pen for the lines then paint with watercolor. Add colored inks to the wet paint for interest.

splat-a-fact

Geckos are the only lizards that have a voice.

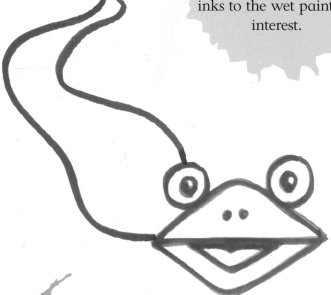

3 Draw in a wiggly body shape.

4 Add legs and splayed feet. Draw in markings on the body.

Parrot

1

Start by drawing the head shape. Add a dot for the eye.

3 Draw in the wings and tail feathers.

Splat-a-fact

There are more than 350 different kinds of parrots.

2 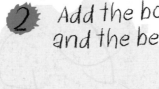 Add the body and the beak.

4 Add the feet and perch.

5 Draw in the feathers.

you can do it!
Add color with watercolor paint. Use felt-tip markers for the lines.

Rabbit

1 Start by drawing a circle for the head.

2 Add ears.

you can do it!

Use oil pastels and smudge them with your finger. Use a felt-tip marker for the lines.

3 Draw in the eyes, nose, mouth, teeth, and whiskers.

4 Add a rounded body and two back feet.

5 Draw in the front legs and paws.

Rat

1 Start with the head shape. Add a dot for the eye.

2 Draw in two ears, a nose, mouth, and whiskers.

3 Draw in the body.

4 Draw in the two back legs.

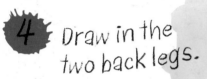

5 Draw in the front legs and a tail. Add toes to each foot.

you can do it!

Draw the lines with a felt-tip marker and then add color with watercolor paint.

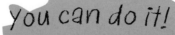

Snake

1 Start by drawing this head shape.

2 Add dots for the eyes and nostrils.

3 Draw in the mouth, and add a forked tongue.

4 Draw a long, curving body.

you can do it!
Draw the lines with a felt-tip marker and use torn tissue paper for color.

5 Add a diamond-shaped pattern.

24

stick insect

1 Start with the head shape. Add dots for eyes.

2 Add two antennae and pincer shapes under the head.

3 Draw in the stick insect's body.

4 Add three legs and feet to each side.

Spider

splat-a-fact

Spiders have eight legs and two body parts: the abdomen and the thorax.
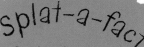

1 Start by drawing two overlapping circles for the head and body.

2 Add four dots for the eyes and two fangs.

3 Draw in three legs on each side.

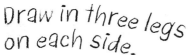

you can do it!
Color the picture with crayons. First place different textured surfaces under the paper to create interesting effects.

4 Add two more front legs.

Tortoise

you can do it!
Color in with watercolor paint. Use a felt-tip marker for the lines.

1 Start with an oval shape for the shell.

2 Add a pattern to the shell. Draw in another curved line around the shell's base.

3 Draw in the head, and add an eye, mouth, and nostrils.

4 Add four legs and a pointed tail.

Splat-a-fact
Tortoises have a protective shell around their body.

30

Index